# How does God Listen?

**KAY LINDAHL,** author of *The Sacred Art of Listening*
Photo illustrations by Cynthia Maloney

*Walking Together, Finding the Way*
SKYLIGHT PATHS Publishing
Woodstock, Vermont

2005 First Printing
Text © 2005 by Kay Lindahl
Photos © 2005 by Cynthia Maloney

**Library of Congress Cataloging-in-Publication Data**
Lindahl, Kay, 1938–
How does God listen? / Kay Lindahl ; full-color photographs by Cynthia Maloney.
p. cm.
ISBN 1-59473-084-9 (pbk.)
1. God—Juvenile literature. 2. Listening—Religious aspects—Juvenile literature. I. Maloney, Cynthia. II. Title.
BL629.5.L57L55 2005
202'.11—dc22

2004026202

10  9  8  7  6  5  4  3  2  1
Manufactured in China

The publisher gratefully acknowledges Reverend August Gold as the inspiration for this series.

Grateful acknowledgment is given for permission to print the following photographs: © Lise Gagne (p. 5), © Andrei Tchernov (p. 6–7), © Debi Bishop (p. 14), © Gintautas Tumulis (p. 17), © David Stead (p. 20), © Ronda Oliver (p. 24), © Russell Warris (p. 26), all courtesy of www.istockphoto.com; and © 2004 by Ron Contrady (p. 18).

SkyLight Paths Publishing is creating a place where people of different spiritual traditions come together for challenge and inspiration, a place where we can help each other understand the mystery that lies at the heart of our existence.

SkyLight Paths sees both believers and seekers as a community that increasingly transcends traditional boundaries of religion and denomination—people wanting to learn from each other, *walking together, finding the way.*

SkyLight Paths, "Walking Together, Finding the Way" and colophon are trademarks of LongHill Partners, Inc., registered in the U.S. Patent and Trademark Office.

*Walking Together, Finding the Way*
Published by SkyLight Paths Publishing
A Division of LongHill Partners, Inc.
Sunset Farm Offices, Route 4, P.O. Box 237
Woodstock, VT 05091
Tel: (802) 457-4000    Fax: (802) 457-4004
www.skylightpaths.com

When I talk to God, is GOD LISTENING TO ME?

Of course, my precious one,

God is always

listening to you.

# How do I know that God is listening?

I can't SEE God.

Well, there are lots of things we can't see,
yet we know they are there.

Think about the wind.
Can you see the wind?

NO.

How do you know
that wind is there?

I can see the leaves
and branches moving
in the trees.

God is like that, too.
Even though we can't see God,
there *are* many signs
that GOD IS LISTENING TO US.


These signs come to us in all kinds of ways—
through what we **touch**, **hear**, *see*,
*taste*, *smell*, and *feel*.

We know God is listening

# when we feel the touch...

of water on our bodies,

sunshine on our faces,

snow on our tongues,

or hugs and kisses from our moms and dads.

We know God is listening

# when we hear...

the whistle of a train carrying family and friends,

the siren of a fire truck,

the purring of a cat,

or Mommy's "good night" whisper
before we fall asleep.

We know God is listening

when we see . . .

spider webs sparkling in the sunlight,

the bright colors of a rainbow,

red and yellow leaves in the fall,

or birds flying in the sky.

We know God is listening

when we taste...

crunchy popcorn,

cold ice cream,

whipped cream in hot chocolate,

or the sweet and sour of lemonade.

We know God is listening

# when we smell...

cookies baking,

the odor of a *skunk,*

the scent of perfume,

or **roses** in the garden.

We know God is listening

WhEn we feel...

our hearts beating,

happiness and laughter,

sadness and tears,

or scared and
alone.

Oh, now I understand.

We know how
God listens to us

just like we know that
God loves us.

Yes, love is something we cannot see
and yet we know it's there.

God loves me
   all the time,

   So God is listening
   to me all the time,

      even when I'm not
      talking to God.

Yes, God is always listening.